Yassa Massa

Tee Hopewell

Presentation by *BookLeaf Publishing*

Web: www.bookleafpub.com

E-mail: info@bookleafpub.com

ISBN: 9789358734706

First edition 2023

DEDICATION

I'd like to dedicate this to my son, Tobias, my father, Melvin, my grandmother, Carrie Mae, as well as myself,

Latoshia Carrie. One is only as good as their muse.

I'd like to also dedicate this to my wife, Britney alongside our daughter Skylar, and our son Tobias. Without their constant support and faith in me and all my dreams, I wouldn't be the version of me that I absolutely love. We have our four beautiful pets, O'Malley, Bentley, Iris, and Sweets that kept me company on days or nights I endured writer's block.

ACKNOWLEDGEMENT

I'd love to pour appreciation and love into all of my friends and family that have always been there and encouraged me. A special nod to my longest friend, Al CHNM. Without all the people in my life and those I met along the way, be it in college friends that become family (KitKat) or elsewhere in life (Melissa) I truly wouldn't enjoy life half as much without you all remaining a steady and constant part of my life.

All in all each and every single person in my life whether mentioned here or not has impacted it in some way that caused inspiration in some capacity for words to be spilled on paper and that will always be held to the highest degree of appreciation from me, despite the journey.

Thank you all for every single thing you've done and things you aren't even aware of. I have appreciated it all and you all.

Remember your worth.

PREFACE

Yessa Massa is a mini-collection of poetry that touches on racial inequality, perspectives, and discrimination. It is an attempt to allow voices to be heard that haven't been previously due to delivery, and/or those that feel unheard while speaking from rooftops. It holds some hard truths within its pages and can be challenging to read, but also offers a crisp view and wish-filled promises of all life should have to offer and all that life tries to stunt.

Restoration

Unconfessed- not convicted - unapologetic;
Still we grab hands that have more power than
we do so that we show the world equality.
Show the world we too want to call it home,
though we have never really entered through the
front door.
Death is a known end result of life;
however marching to death should not be part of
the stains we allow on our hands.
Filled with buts and false justifications of
wrongful blood taken;

Vomiting up every excuse as if that helps wipe
that slate clean.
Do you see what is wrong with that logic?
That statement?
This isn't guilt-free indulgence,
but counting lives has become as popular as
counting calories when one wants to flex.
So here I kneel stretching;
trying to stand against the systematic epidemic
spreading through the nation.
Praying that the UNITED in our name catches
like wildfire
instead of lighting like a wet flame; crackles,
sparks.
Only to refuse the ignition of the authority.
You understand?
That's diving in deep without knowing how to
swim,
yet not for lack of trying.
I am not moving to separate,
but to generate others to participate in stopping
hate so we all don't decimate from the egregious
states of the ongoing mind activity,
though we can't seem to relate.
Now as one voice; unconfessed, not convicted,
unapologetic—
Yet never unforgiving and never unforgettable.

Don't Shoot

Hands up to block, to protect, to fight, to
surrender.
Hands up, feet planted.
To stand, to fall, to clear our names;
To show mercy, to show innocence, to show no
threat is being made.
Hands up to catch, to help, to receive, to give;
Hands up, arms tired, knees buckling.
Hands up to show skin color on the inside of the
palm;
Hands up just for everyone else to see the outer
casing.
Hands up to show we too bleed the same color.

Hands up to become a part of the society we live
in;
A part of society we surrender to;
A part of the people we fight for;
A part of the people we die for;
A part of the people that kill us.
Hands up to embrace the skin we live in.
To walk proudly as a black man, to walk proudly
as a black woman.
Hands up to defend our honor, to defend our
integrity, to defend our race.
Hands up to defend those that come against, to
embrace the very people who shoot us down;
Hands up to defend our own people who shoot
us down.
Hands up to the crack of the whip,
to the crack of the gun,
to the cracks of the cuffs.
Hands up to plead to live;
to announce our glory;
to announce our victories,
and to announce our failures.
Hands up to embrace ... just to embrace.
Hands up, steps forward;
And though we stand in eye view --
We have never emerged from the shadows.

Overlay

Written off- buried;
No trace of the footsteps of dragging feet;
If you will;
Left behind as I struggled for life.
Struggled to live in the world we call home,
Even after demons have tried to wipe us from
existence--
And still it continues.
The blind eye turned so as not to witness the
whips received daily.

Denying it because the crack of the whip can no
longer be heard
We no longer abuse them they say;
We no longer cage them they say;
Remember when they say;
When is and always has been present;
labeled as a bad name even after lending hands.
Have we not lent our souls enough,
or do you beg us to give you more than our
souls?
Either way you will always see one shade.
Remember that when you cannot take the heat.

Hi-Fi

The saying is a house divided cannot stand --
What happens when we forget the house
altogether,
and take to the nation instead.
When we allow narrowed minds to keep the fist
of power;
because those that could have—
rejected any knowledge of the depressed
dynamics the world displayed-
And counted sheep as a ruse to being awake.
A strong voice we obtain.

but if it doesn't pour out like milk,
regardless of whether it's curdled,
it is no longer heard.
Movements to be discovered,
to be considered someone that matters;
without providing our papers to show that we
are permitted to do so.
Our hardened exterior is only present
due to the prejudiced perspiration dripping with
pain,
and mishandling to all this bigotry.
The humor in everything being even despite
belonging to the captured group,
it is not our minds that need to be liberated.
Instead of hatred we hold onto higher
intellectual frequencies that remain permanent
inside
and cause each step we take to be a step toward
the very thing that every color in the box is
striving for...

The American Dream

Transparent

When fog is thick and present, seeing becomes a challenge, but there in that very challenge is another prison.

It's blindingly luminous in all its blanketed
identity.
I do not condemn you because you prefer cream
and sugar in yours;
In saying that do not condemn me because I
accept mine black.
It is not a jab or to undermine universal lives-
It is difference;
And that becomes a beautiful scene when similar
ground is still stood upon even without a solid
foundation.
Palms touch skin not color,
Hearts see souls not shades;
But even in saying that do not deny who you are
to fill part of who you aren't.
Don't release where you have been to feel whole
to where you haven't.
Is weak the new strong?
Is silence the forever loud?
Questions that will never be answered because
though I am independent as an American;
I stay imprisoned in actions I do not understand.
Slavery two point Oh..
Difficulty processing;
That though fog and darkness occur in the world
differently;
They are both still allowed existence.
Are you still with me?

Tit for Tat

Only allowed the light that is given.
Wanted.
Entertainment-
The illumination provided.
Brawn, no brains.
That's shackled shouting.
Shrill voices erupt-
Some, stained.
Others- smudged.
Many: cascading waterfalls- refreshing to the
soul.

And if the spotlight wasn't tracking,
If participation wasn't scrutinized with fear of impairment;
A life similarly lived might be found-
But every move needs to be known,
And that's not a tennis skill.
More of a shot-put.
And cannon balls are locked and loaded.
Manned armory ready to battle,
Unaware some of the artillery was swiped;
Many previously opposing soldiers have linked arms with the enemy,
And on the end of publicized fingers; those that lack the preferred clarity;
Their war only allowed the light that is given.

Poison Picking

As long as I hold my tongue I am accepted;
For every time I am docile I am authorized to
go.
So long as I turn away from the wrath set before
instead of bringing my own thought of an
extinguisher I am not eliminated.
I am forced to be color blind,
Just wait let me go further in.
I am required to dissociate with my background;
my race;
Else I hate others;

I am terrorized to not stand up for the inequality
that is put on display--
Like it is the best seller because if I do I become
"part of the problem."
I have no say when that excessive force is being
used on me because then I am a criminal.
I am labeled as a thug if I stand up to wrongful
convictions;
And resist undeserved actions.
Yet the end result is the same if I do exactly
what is said of me.
Regardless; I stand wholly me
While that very same land exercises their right
to freely kill with no repercussions.
Silence is slapped onto every malpractice for the
sake of character and position,
Comparatively it is cuffed onto me as a warning
shot for my observant truth to become absent of
sound.
No other way to remain tied to the land of
chances if it's regurgitated onto tribunals of
peacemakers,
Just for peace to kiss me as I take my last breath.
An eternity of waiting and still an eternity to go-
Before the past will pass and the idea of one
nation will take place of the fallen bodies that
cry out for justice.
My refusal might secure my demise,
But at least it will be at my own expense.

Instruction Manual

Be close to home long before the streetlights
come on,
And don't have your hood up when walking
anywhere.
'Cause eyes are always watching.
Hands at ten and two if red and blue lights up
your rear view.
Manners to those that don't even deserve it;
'Cause you were taught better.

Know it's not your shoulders humanity has hung
hate on.
They have some kind of diseased areas within
them,
No cure.
Be a sponge in a storm;
Soaking up every inch of knowledge you may
later be denied.
The upstairs must stay tidy too, so sweep and
check the cobwebs don't attract crawling inside
the mind.
Watch your mouth when it works so it's not
witchcraft whispering.
Praise as much as you can so those hands stay
visible;
Meeting the maker happens one way;
Though many think they are the maker
themselves.
Though those legs will carry you places;
Restrict your stroll.
Keep those freedom feet from running,
'Cause chasing is a favorite pastime.
Keep that backbone strong;
But resist the programmed reaction to
detainment.
Mind control with a waltz and use the language
of your sway;
Speak sweet, saturated words through clenched
teeth-

And yes I know poison never tastes good,
But air isn't free.
And carry that solace everywhere;
At all times you'll need a shelter-
Finding it within is your only guarantee in this
life.
Build accordingly.

Camp Follower

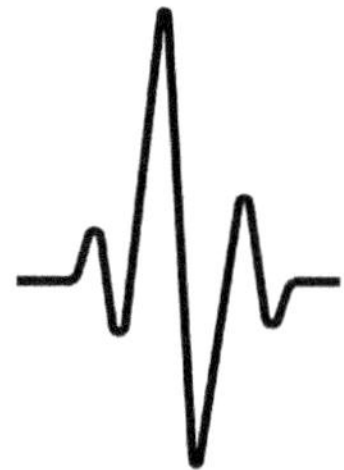

Taking away any hope of having a normal life is
where the mind is seized,
but we know better.
Enclosed in a fence that we built-
Centuries of captivity only awaken the legs to
stand-
To push-
Unaware of adaptations to the roles they beg us
to play-
To areas they allow us to reside in;

This early exposure to hatred will not stay
engrained.
We are the overseers of our own souls;
Still they search for us as if this is a warped
Hide and seek match,
Evidence of detachment shows as they continue
Knocking knees knowingly that this cannot
possibly be the way-
They do not even know that the more they
reveal-
The more they act-
The more hate they spread-
The fewer that continue to blindly follow along.
Trauma does not keep us down-
After all they try to beat us to the end of our
lives;
But when did blood ever come from stone?

My Own Recollection

Beaten souls run the flesh from beating hearts.
The content of character unseen, unheard,
unimportant;
Distances traveled due to whip cracks,
Due to false color deficit eyes,
Attributed to detestable diction overlaying every
eyelid;
Every ounce of framework yet,
Unnoticed.

A foreigner in the house built by hands that
belong to us too.
Doors made to actually separate instead of
enclose us all together.
What is the reasoning for this?
Still reexamining the tactics we are using
because it is unfathomable;
Why we step into the same past footprints we
used before.
The outcome known;
and still this path seems right yet again.
We detach ourselves from the previous hurt we
witnessed;
and we chalk it up to being in consequence-
of savage behavior—
that was acted upon-
But fail to see the savageness of the route that
was chosen repeatedly leads to the already
prepared stage for act two;
revealing that the claim of us being so far ahead
than where we once were
Is a misconception provided to us by the many
producers that drift in and out making sure the
lanes stay clear of actual freedom.

Ascension

So look up,
Or look down.
Whichever causes your downcast away from my
horizons;
As peacekeeper and judge over this ruling
temple -
You have no gavel here.
All rise;
Tis now upon my own order.

Injustice

The faces it's plagued, evident.
Not all the same shade;
As the world would have you believe.
Some moonlit … struggling to understand these
confines-
Others soot stricken: denied common courtesy
for giving exactly that;
Common courtesy
Occasionally; one will find freedom fighters;
Using every weapon, save good intentions, to
define the stance.

The tongues all speak at once;
And only a handful understand what's been
offered at all times.
"A melting pot"
Stirred by bleached bones.
Prepared by muddied accomplices.
Yielded by those that are just trying to get by;
Individuals looking in on themselves;
Trying to find the stains that earned them this
stay.
And they're not the only ones.

Risen

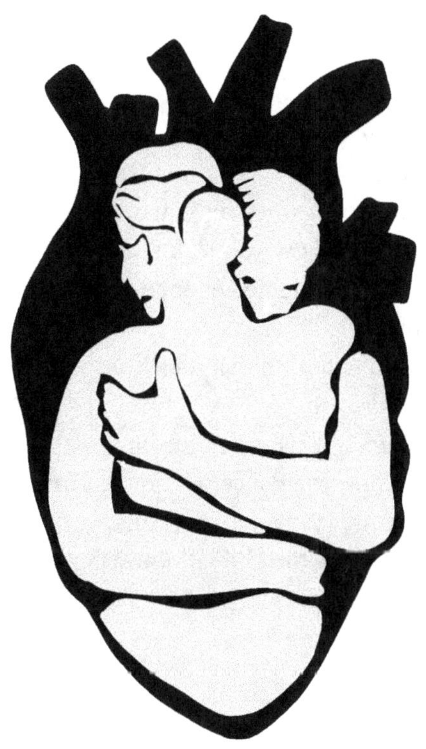

Oh, how you must be of vital importance;
To take the entire whole of another human

And define them as nothing-
Due to their reflection not making that of the one
you see in your own mirror;
The upset so poisonous;
So dangerous.
Duplicate the assessed indignation;
The plan of attack.
As far as it went too.
Forget having an end game.
Stop them.
And them being whoever you aren't.
Yes; goodness how you leek relevance-
Your opinion weighted enough to attempt
becoming rule.
Holds so much girth that it cavities the minds of
others;
Herds them to perform accordingly-
All the while you dance within the virus.
Knowing the toxins will find their way in.
Indeed, you are the only all-knowing crusader;
And we… the people.

Two-Sided Coin

I see you;
despite the thought process pre-programmed:
Hard wired.
And I want to hold you-

But you have been predisposed to knowing no
weapon formed against . . .
And I am that weapon.
All chiseled bone;
Lacking sharp edges.
The same danger they pretend to be in;
Seen in my eyes as they try to catch and hold
your stare.
And I know you;
Hated for everything you stand for;
Everything you don't.
Same grass in this yard.
But you're a stranger still;
And though we've met,
We've never actually been able to encounter
each other.
Though we've talked;
We've never actually conversed.
The similarities define our differences;
Cast us into a spotlight;
Not belonging to us.
Not even lent,
But illuminating all the same.
And we stand there;
My mind on you staying-
Yours on running.
Able to see;
But unable to-
Comprehend.

Search Lights

And if at any time you ever allow yourself to
open up-
and rearrange your thoughts so that they differ
from all the spoon-fed lessons gathered for;
If ever you find yourself standing in the middle
of a choice-
With voices commanding you back from which
you came,
And nothing convincing you to push forward;

If any moment you fall into-
gifts a moment of pause from the failsafe ways
that you know,
And holds back from direction pointing;
Would you change the shadows to know me?
And if so-
Would you then run from the spotlight that may
follow?

A League of My Own

A light patch here.
A dark swoop there.
Marked by birth across most of the surface
What went untouched; the best of all worlds,
But the flaw pointed out.
The index never the same though-
Often times; decolorized and accusing-
And insult to injury; coppered and rejective.
No space on either side of the tracks-
The thought process being that belonging is even
desired;

Rare to see anything one can even attach to
within these open-aired walls surrounding . . .

Except for division.

ALM

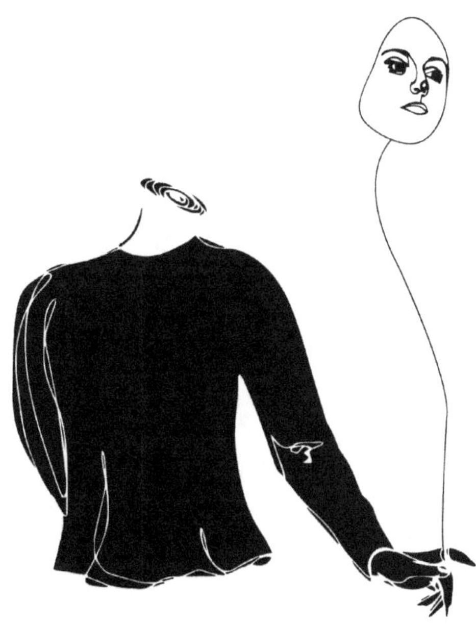

As if we didn't matter.
The spotlight; black and white.
All else printed falls to the outskirts,
Without lacking the headline.
Any inquiry for it to read as front page;
Seemingly insensitive.
Problems known and problems seen.
Solutions don't sell as well;
And rage swells with the right push.
So silence then,
As if we didn't matter.

Give up?

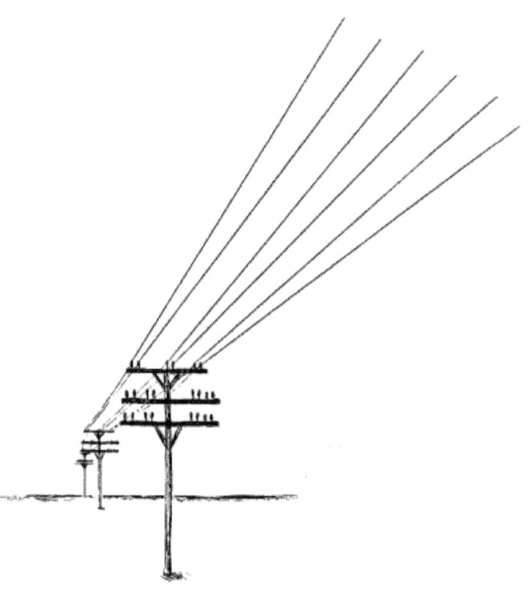

The shadows stay comforting;
But suffocating.
Trying to puppet without being seen;
And also trying to shine.
Impossible to have it both ways;
Yet efforts pour through these hands.
Sand molds from previous safety steps and still;
Dangerous to live.
Dangerous to hide.
Dangerous to die;

All the while the encouragement stings the skin
when it lands-

Rise to the challenge!
The omitted truth: just to rot from the attempt.

Recite

Each time I think I am less than;
And all the moments that have passed that held
me feeling worthless-
Every time I caught myself enduring the way
lyrics crooned from rotted teeth--
As if that made the bitter taste better -
when the cup brought forth met mouth.
And the blow as degrading as being shackled to
slap;

Without the skin marks.
The soul bleeds all the same.
Unable to decode the issue-
And uprooting views seems as useless as is
thought of me.
So hate? Ignorance?
The answer as popular as conversations on the
subject matter.
Wool covers the sheep that fail to see the subject
matter stays continuous-

To define us; home of the brave while you stay
land of the free.

On the swivel

Meticulous.
That's engrained early on.
Intentional.
Every step must be considered.
Every decision calculated.
Born into controlled freedom;
Due to one misstep determining my character.
Maintain every concept of "stand-up citizen"
And experience little your peers do.
To copy brings the cat-
And we, the mice, are seen as the leading
offense.
Grouped together and eradicated-
Bullied into closed spaces where the deed can be
done-
No flexing-
The misconception -
We behave as rodents.
So march on-
Stay deliberate.
Diligent.
Decisive.
Remaining everything you are,
And nothing they've tried to define,
but instead labeled you.

Congregation

I move like honey on Sundays;
Slow and sweet.
A rock me softly tune.
Molasses melody.
The ebony pulling people of all shades in;
And on Monday's it's pop;
In or out, and still always both.
Back and forth movement,
Devoid of seesaw waves.
Turbulent.
High frequency.
Tuesday's; gospel lessons.
All big-bodied energy on full display.
Bass drums on perfect beat;
Sole slapping success riddles throughout the day.

Wednesday's garage made cadence;
Pointed and roaring-
Only an idea at the end of the hands being the
incentive,
But littered with souls, surface to floor, all the
same.
Thursday is world-weary.
Arms strained;
Just enough to seem open, but actually
detaining.
Force-fed flavors never asked for, but offered
without prompting.
Country counting the Friday's.
Tongue-tied and round-a-bouts;
Finding all the lives on that highway-
They all reveled in years ago.
Sightseeing Saturdays allow crows feet to just
land-
Knowledge behind the lens that captured new
horizons.
Bristling nights;
filled with full-throated, long-held notes.
Captioning the lyrics here, but the genre unfixed.

Weighted Blanket

Bated breath caused anxiety to crawl and weave
around my voice box; choking off
the supply of words I had prepared specifically
for them. I looked into eyes that
held me hostage –
eyes that I would have done anything for, given
anything to --
Eyes that knew they were slowly killing me --
and allowed each fatal blow to land.
And they know the comfort they offer when I
am lying face down in the dirt only
further strangles me --
They know the embrace burns my skin --

but the security they were donating was for their
own satisfaction instead --
And I've never been one to find my tongue after
I've assisted in cutting it out.
Every time I swear to myself that I will matter
more than the obligation to return
a similar frame of mind -- reciprocate the
invasion of personal space --
Match the empty emotion put forth --
I always walk away with abandoned hands.

Raincoat

She's awake -- but refuses to open her windows.
She knows what's waiting just beyond her
eyelids -- the flaws that will pronounce
themselves strongly as soon as she gives in to
awareness.
It's hard to stand in the mirror and see that she
doesn't even fit in her reflection.
There is no safe haven for her to escape to -- and
the arms she has to choose from
are hollow in all the areas she needs to be
touched.

The sheets coiled around her body are the
closest thing to a hug -- that isn't
dripping with expectations -- she'll ever receive
--
and she doesn't even enjoy the suffocation of an
embrace --
but she also hates being cold --
and she can't explain through her chattering teeth
what she wants to feel or why
she wants to hide just in case someone wants to
find her --
so her lips hold each other, and her eyes slightly
open to pull her out of the
darkness and into the light --
that still blinds her
and ruins any hope she had of seeing the bright
side.

Barefoot

She cannot find the right words to describe it --
they all seem too heavy, too busy. Her feelings
mirror the void expression on their
face --
the emptiness in their chest. She is filled with
questions of who she is, why she is,
what she is --
and there is no answer in sight. She has made a
life adopting titles and trying to
force herself to fit the frames she handpicked,
but her touch was never delicate,
and her drive was no stranger to failure --
Still she watches as the flesh rips from the soles
of her feet as she leaves her
footprints behind in search of anything that will
reveal a purpose --
a path --

an idea that she can follow.
She has attempted to create her own, but her
mind is stuck in a loop of
insignificancy and her soul is anchored to all
that she thinks of herself -- nothing.

Marionette

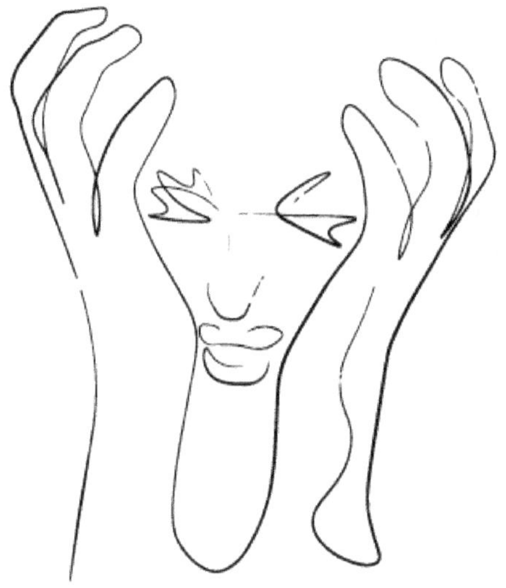

A slice visible – reachable; still to be
determined.
Slivers too shallow to attempt slipping through.
Senses topsy-turvy;
Throwing any hope of blending in out into the
wind -
A breeze the skin is desperate to feel,
But deterred from physical touch.
Numb to the outer edges that pool within;
Deep shades of all the negative nuances that
echo -

That puppet;
That are always swimming in the iris –
Obstructing any clarity that may come.
Fingers spread wide;
All the cracks being held together with the tips –
Curling at the hairline –
Trying to stop the messy beliefs.
My – how the palms that cradled the cheeks –
That smiled pain down themselves –
Have tightened into captivity.

Stoicism

Not all obstacles; abrasive claps; Require
continuous commandments – Drawn
out demands.
Space becomes shut down if met with dangerous
foundations posing as safety
zones. Feelings possibly void – Possibly
suppressed; Maybe even misunderstood
– So unknown. Trying to hide - Sweeping away
may only deceive the public
momentarily. Shadows lighten; The sun will
illuminate – The moon will cause
blush-speckled rays to become spotlights – To
the hurdles trying to be left

behind. Though, at the same time ignored. The
desire for a melody map turned
up – deafening to any other sense outside of the
ability to hear the toxic waste
threatening to spill out and finish this spiral.
Pretending the poison that pollutes
any idea of positivity simply doesn't exist. Out
of sight - out of mind - but never
out of earshot. Forced to replay the same rock to
the ever-changing rolls as
another strike illuminates all that lies ahead,
most of what's followed behind, and
the beautiful, unfulfilling, delicate nightmare
that appreciation conditions.

Railroad

Captured - the main describing term bottled up
and offered biweekly. Unlike the

air, purified might I add, greedily sucked into
your lungs; and the space you allow.
Unaware at any time I may remember the
heights I can achieve. Controlled.
Floodlights strengthen the desire for order -
attention then weakens - the fine line
between complete neglect and slight efforts in
danger of root rot. Unable to drain
diseased soil despite my swiss army brain
sending problem-solving anxiety into
overdrive. Elevated, but reaching.

Homemade

First gather all the vital parts --
of yourself that will certainly determine the
finished product --
Add in a pinch of light
A heaping pour of silver tongue
A dash of compassion
A healthy amount of sarcasm
Overflow it with humor --
Because the heart will need a defense
mechanism--
And allow it to sit in the dark --

As you allowed me --
Groom it until it's finally time for it to take its
steps.
Encourage it to find how to become something
more --
And when it finally rises to the occasion --
Break it as you broke me.
We all know you enjoy pieces scattered rather
than something whole.

Grizzly

Maybe I'm undeserving --
It's possible pollution has filled my soul deeply,
and is now seeping from my pores --
And maybe that's what deters them.
The stains in my heart contaminated enough to
be unworthy of even a
child's undelayed affection --
And how do I fix what I've yet to understand?
Why does my eagerness to connect fall on
deaf ears --
mute mouths --

caged hearts --
and bite back at me?
Venom fangs.
And how do you hold liquid close to your chest
when your hands are a
useless flask?
And how do you let go of the idea that anyone
will see you as someone
worth protecting?

Cyclonic

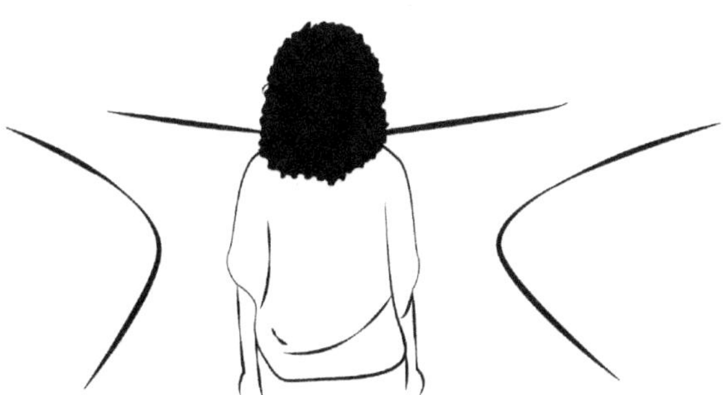

Hate is -- like lava coming down and absorbing
everything – everyone.
Filling in their empty creases and then spewing
from them -- in a similar
fashion that it did from the mouths of the source,
and we never really know
who that source is when it's metaphorical like
this -- rooted in the same
spot -- knowing the pain of the burn -- knowing
it'll melt my bones into
ashes and that I'll have to build myself back up
-- just to relive the trauma.
And I do. I stand for those who cannot -- who
can and won't out of fear or
shame -- the weak-minded individuals. The
opinionated, yet low-voiced
beings -- the backbone recoveries -- the
voiceless, and all the in-betweens

-- yet somewhere along the way I quit standing
up for myself. Shame on you
self, how dare you value others over your own
flesh and blood.

Hotfoot

I'm stuck -
I'm stuck and they are rushing me.
Rushing and banging on the only protection
between them and myself -
Protection that isn't truly protection in my eyes,
but instead a weapon if broken.
A weapon like me -
broken like me -
Me; still exactly in the place I was installed
originally -
Original; yet predetermined ideas keep me
predictable -
predictable unlike the dreams that awaken my
courage -

Courage that dissipates as soon as my eyes see
any amount of light.
Light; the one thing that makes me
uncomfortable -
Uncomfortable because I can be seen